Get Confident

and

Accelerate Your Career

Caroline Arnold

Dedication

I'd like to thank my partner, my family and my friends for all their support.

Thanks go too to the many amazing people that I've met networking and who have inspired me to follow my dreams.

And to all the women out there who pick up this book and are inspired to get confident and accelerate their career. I thank you for having the courage to fulfil your potential and make a difference in the world.

I would love to hear how you get on.

Contents

Section 1

Introduction

Why am I writing this book?

When I was fifteen I read a book called 'The Hotel on the Roof of the World: 5 years in Tibet'. That book inspired me to be a hotel owner at some point in the future.

Aged 15, and in pursuit of my dream, I secured a summer job in a hotel doing everything from waitressing and being a chambermaid to manning reception. The manager promised to show me the different areas of the hotel's operations in order to give me a flavour of what went into running a hotel. I was so excited.

But two weeks later I ran home in tears after this same manager told me if I touched the toaster again he would cut my fingers off as that was his job.

Granted, I was a somewhat sensitive fifteen-year-old but this wasn't the introduction into the working world I'd expected or hoped for.

He was the first boss I left due to a poor management style but he wasn't the last. In fact, it got worse, a lot worse, before I encountered the best boss I could have ever have had. That boss supported me and helped me achieve my potential and complete my graduate programme several years later.

One of the reasons for writing this book is in the hope of helping those of you currently struggling with the boss from hell. If just one woman reading feels inspired to make that move then it will have been worthwhile.

I followed the typical path of a young women leaving school in 2000: I went off to university to study Economics and Business.

Post-graduation I took a gap year. I worked for six months before travelling around Asia, Australia and America for a further six months. On my return, I embarked on a graduate programme with a well-known retail brand and went on to have a successful career in Human Resources for large global corporate organizations.

But by 2015 I knew it was time to be true to the calling I felt to be my own boss. I'd worked in the corporate environment for over a decade. That experience meant I related to the difficulties that women faced not only from their employers but also from their own internal challenges as they tried to progress in their careers.

I have a vision where equality is not an issue. One where there are an equal number of men and women in senior management roles. One where young girls don't think that business studies is a subject for the boys.

We owe it to ourselves and to those that came before us and fought for the right to vote and for equal pay. There's still a lot of work to do to achieve equality in the boardroom and pay parity. And so it's our responsibility to the next generation to work towards that. We shouldn't limit them by our actions – or our inactions - now.

It's my firm belief that all women deserve to be happy and to reach their full potential both at work and in their personal lives. It's frustrating to hear that someone isn't happy but unclear what to do to turn their situation around. Or, even if they do know, they feel too petrified to speak up or to leave a stable job.

The aim of this book is to give you practical tips. Tips to help you increase your confidence and gain greater clarity on what it is that you want in your career. Then you'll know what steps you need to take to accelerate it.

There are exercises throughout the book designed to help you get this clarity, to increase your confidence and then, when you're ready, to accelerate your career.

So, let's start with the first exercise below.

Exercise 1
Why have you picked up this book?

1.
2.
3.

Exercise 2
What don't you feel now, that you want to feel at the end of this book?

1.
2.
3.

Who is this book for?

This book is for all women who are working or wish to return to work and who want to become more confident and accelerate their career. Whether that's to become the best marketing manager for a small local charity or to secure their first board appointment.

If any of these statements resonate then this book is for you.

1. Your school teachers told you that you wouldn't amount to anything so there was no point in going to university.

2. You're a female graduate just embarking on your career.

3. You're returning to work after a career break and feel worried about how on earth you'll manage everything.

4. You want to be more confident in your personal and professional life.

5. You feel you've lost your sparkle, you have Sunday blues and dread Monday morning coming around again.

6. You're new to management and want to be an inspiring leader to the rest of your team.

7. You enjoy self-development books with practical tips that you can put into practice straight away.

8. You're in a HR team that wants to promote a culture of diversity.

9. You're a female director who wants to inspire the next generation.

This book is also for men with daughters and partners or who manage a team of females so that you have a better understanding of how you can best support the women around you.

How to use this book

There's no right or wrong way to use this book, so which ever feels right for you will be the right way.

Some will prefer to read the book through to get an overview then come back and do the exercises. Others though will prefer to go through the book, doing each exercise as they arise. Trust that how you approach this book will give you everything that you want.

If you've bought this book as a physical book then you can annotate it as you go. Complete the exercises and highlight the sections that you want to return to. That way you won't forget the tip that created an 'Ah ha' moment for you.

Keep this book with you as you go about your day Then, when you find five minutes, while waiting for an appointment say, you can read another chapter or complete an exercise.

If you only spend five minutes a day on the book you'll make steady progress through it. A good motto to remember as you go through it is 'progress not perfection'.

As you work through the exercises you may decide to take your time to think about each question. Once you get an idea or two the rest will follow. If nothing comes immediately don't worry - move on and come back to that section later.

But do come back to it!

There are lots of practical tips in this book. Some of them you'll resonate with the moment you read them and want to put into action straight away.

Others though may not be so relevant for you right now. That doesn't matter. This is a book that you can return to as your life circumstances change.

The chapters are short on purpose. That way, if you've only got a few minutes each day to read you'll be able to read a chapter and start implementing that chapter during the day.

Should you have purchased the 'Get Confident and Accelerate Your Career' online programme then this book will complement the activities as you work through the course. If you haven't bought the online programme then I invite you to have a look at the course on my website: www.carolinearnoldcoaching.com

If you haven't yet connected with me on my social media platforms then please feel free to do that now.

Exercise 3
Connect and follow me on Social Media:

1. LinkedIn   linkedin.com/in/carolinearnoldcoach
2. Website   www.carolinearnoldcoaching.com
3. Twitter   @Carnoldcoaching
4. Facebook   https://m.facebook.com/Carolinearnoldcoaching
5. Instagram https://www.instagram.com/carolinearnoldcoaching/

Section 2

Get Confident

What confidence is

When I do presentations on confidence in companies to an audience of women I always ask the question: 'what does confidence mean to you'.

The responses I get vary. So take a moment to think about this question and write down three things that come to your mind when you think of confidence.

Exercise 4
What does confidence mean to me?

1.
2.
3.

For me, confidence is that belief in oneself, a willingness to express one's view and a feeling that you can do anything.

Confidence is being able to take on challenges at work while feeling supported by colleagues. Then if you do make a mistake, well that's okay so long as you put your hand up and learn from it.

Confidence is feeling that you can speak up and be listened to. It enables you to seek out opportunities and helps you wake up and stand tall.

Recently I gave a talk on 'Confidence and Women in the Workplace'. At the end of the talk someone asked, 'can you be confident in everything?' This is such a great and relevant question. We women have our own understanding of 'having it all' and have great expectations and pressure put upon us by society.

We're expected to have the perfect bikini body, be eating a clean diet and producing home cooked dinners all the while being a director, owning a beautiful home and having the perfect relationship with everyone. I don't know about you but just thinking about all of that makes me feel tired and overwhelmed.

So, can we be confident in everything and, more importantly, should we want or even need to be?

I don't think we can be confident in everything but feel we shouldn't aspire to it. The day I feel that I'm confident in every aspect of my life is the day I need to give myself a stern talking to. Because then I'll know I've stopped trying to grow and learn and expand my comfort zone.

If you want to, you can acquire confidence in anything you set your mind to. But that first time you try something you'll probably be nervous and your inner voice or imposter syndrome feeling may well try to sabotage your success.

If you think about five things that you're confident about now and think back to when you first did them – well I bet you didn't feel so self-assured about any of them then.

Exercise 5
Write down five things that you're confident in now:

1.
2.
3.
4.
5.

If I think back to the first time I interviewed someone, the first time I went for an interview, the first time I wrote a blog, sent my first tweet or did my first triathlon – I definitely wasn't confident.

In fact, far from it!

However, I gave them all a go. I then thought about how I could improve and learn from the experience so that I'd do it better the next time.

Through my coaching, I've found that women, as a general rule, aren't naturally as confident as men. This tends to be due to one or more of the challenges below.

- **Pre-conditioned beliefs:** Women can feel that men are more confident or are better at certain tasks. As a result, they feel they won't be listened to or that they aren't worthy.

- **Male dominated environment**: It remains the case that certain industries are male dominated.

- **Not encouraged to lead:** This could be an historic challenge from when they were at school or university.

- **Lack of experience in speaking out:** Many women have little experience at public speaking or talking in the board room so feel self-conscious when they're called to do so.

- **Recruitment:** The wording in the job description may seem to be more suited to a man's strengths so straight away may put women off.

- **Lack of role model:** some companies still don't have a diverse management team so women coming up the career ladder don't have anyone they can look up to.

Yet it's my firm belief that you can change your mindset and become more confident, enabling you to achieve anything that you want in your professional life.

Think about what you want from your career over the next twelve months and write down three goals. Then keep returning to these goals as you work through this book so that you stay on track to achieve them.

Exercise 6
What 3 goals do you want to achieve in the next 12 months?

1.
2.
3.

Exercise 7
How would feeling more confident help you?

1.
2.
3.

Throughout this section, we're going to focus on different techniques that will help you get confident.

These are tips that I've used at different stages in my life to help me be more confident. Give each one a try even if you've never heard of it or you've tried it before and you didn't feel that it worked for you then. You may be in a different place now so this time it may work! You won't know until you try it.

Turn off your inner voice

We all have an inner voice.

Mine often appears when I am trying to create an Excel spreadsheet. It says 'you hate Excel, don't you remember the last time you tried to add a fancy formula and you had to watch a video on Google on how to do it?'

Yours may speak out when you're about to present to your team, ask for a pay rise or start a new job.

So, what is the inner voice, why is it bad and how do you stop it sabotaging your success?

What is it?
The inner voice, inner critic, negative chatter, inner dialogue, gremlin, intrusive thoughts – whatever you want to call it – it's that voice inside your head that produces feelings of shame, deficiency, low self-esteem, and even depression. It may also cause self-doubt and undermine self-confidence.

Why is it bad?
Whatever you call this thing everyone has one and yours is sabotaging your success in your professional and personal life.

Did you not bother to apply for that job because you couldn't do three out of the ten competencies? Or did you not ask for a pay rise this year because 'you didn't feel worth it?' 'After all', the voice will reason, 'if you were worthy of a pay rise then your employer would surely have given you one?'

Sorry, I hate to burst that bubble but that's just not the way the working world works.

Whenever I give presentations to companies the questions I'm asked most often are about the inner voice and how to deal with it.

Exercise 8
What is your inner voice saying that is sabotaging your success at work?

1.
2.
3.

Try the tips below to stop your inner voice sabotaging your success.

Create an achievements list

Every Friday afternoon I sit down and write down everything I've achieved that week. This reminds me of how much I've managed to get done and puts me in a positive frame of mind for the weekend. It's also a great tool to refer to when you need a confidence boost.

You may also choose to do yours each Friday afternoon. Alternatively, you may want to write down three things that you've achieved as you go to bed so that you're in a positive frame of mind before going to sleep.

I also use an App called '**Five Minute Journal**' which gives me a place to write three things I'm grateful for, three things I will do to make today great and a daily affirmation in the morning. Then at the end of the day I can add a photo of the day and note down three amazing things that happened today. I like that it captures all of this information in one place so that I can easily look back. I recommend downloading the App and trying it for yourself.

Exercise 9
What three things have you achieved in the last week?

1.
2.
3.

Create a gratitude list

This is similar to the achievements list in that you can refer to it if you need a reminder of everything that you have in your life.

I created mine by writing down one hundred things that I was grateful for and I look at it at least twice a week.

You may want to do something similar. Or, at the end of each day, you might write down three things that you're grateful for or sign up to the '**Five Minute Journal App**' and capture this on a daily basis.

Exercise 10
What three things are you grateful for in your life?

1.
2.
3.

Meditation

I don't know about you, but it seems to me that there are so many demands on us fabulous women that sometimes it can all get a bit too much.

I remember in my last corporate job there were times I'd have to go into the toilets, put on my music and do breathing techniques in order to psyche myself up for the rest of the day.

I've found that doing some simple daily meditation with an App such as '**Headspace**' helps to tune out the inner voice. I also use an App called '**Omvana**' and on a monthly basis do the 'Six Phase Meditation'. This helps me get clear on what I want to be doing in my life.

Research has shown that those who practice meditation can have lower anxiety levels, stress and depression and I'd have to agree with this!

Exercise 11
Download '**Headspace**' or another meditation App and schedule it in your diary as a recurring activity.

Positive affirmations

Some people think saying positive affirmations is a little fluffy so they don't try it. But why knock something if you haven't tried it? For me, they are a useful thing to say when that inner voice surfaces. You can tell the inner voice to stop and replace it with a positive affirmation.

You may want to print off a list of positive affirmations and put them somewhere where you'll see them every day. Places like the back of your wardrobe door, or in the bathroom. Or you may just choose one affirmation that you have as a screen saver on your computer.

I do a combination of those and I also add them to my phone. Every hour from eight in the morning to ten at night I have a positive affirmation come up on my phone. This gives me a boost, reminds me of my goal and keeps me in the most positive frame of mind.

Here are some examples that I use:
- My mind has unlimited power
- Progress not perfection
- I am worthy
- I can do anything
- I love and enjoy what I do
- I am committed to my goals
- I am taking action towards my goals
- I am filled with amazing ideas
- Every day I take a step towards becoming more confident
- I am grateful for my family, house, job
- I am grateful for this time
- I create opportunities for myself
- I am open and receptive to anything
- I deserve good things in my life
- I easily find solutions
- I enjoy what I do
- I wake up to the best job
- I am in control of my life
- I relish learning something new
- I am proud of my achievements
- I have the ability to do anything that I want

You can come up with your own affirmations that work for you but use some of the above to start with if you are struggling to think of anything at this stage.

Exercise 12
What three affirmations can you use daily? Add them to your phone as a reminder.
1.
2.
3.

Step outside your comfort zone

Once a week do something that you feel uncomfortable with so that your comfort zone stretches.

If you don't like public speaking put yourself forward at work to do a presentation. Once you've completed it you'll realize it wasn't nearly as scary as you thought it would be. Then the next time you offer to do a presentation, you'll notice your inner voice doesn't appear because you know that you'll be a great success having done it before!

Exercise 13
What three things can you do over the next month to step outside your comfort zone?

1.
2.
3.

Reading

I once attended a conference where the speaker and founder of a multi-million-dollar business said he read a book every week so that he was always learning and stayed ahead of his rivals.

This struck a chord with me as I have always been an avid reader. Although I have to admit I use to read more crime and easy read nonfiction books than anything else.

Since that event though I now read one to two books a week on topics such as personal development, business leadership and being an entrepreneur. I've found this helps me to keep growing as a female business owner, come up with a great list of books as well as develop an ever-growing list of practical ideas for my clients to practice.

Besides which, I find it most therapeutic to sit down in the evening and read a few chapters. And it's a good way to start a conversation with someone if you see them reading a book that you've read.

A lot of people tell me they don't have time to read. If that's you then try delaying turning on the TV or go to bed ten minutes earlier. If you read for ten minutes every day you'll read on average eighteen books a year. That's a lot of books full of ideas and information that can help you get confident and that you can put into practice in your career.

If you'd like a list of suggested books then turn to the back of this book for my recommendations. You can also subscribe to my newsletter via my website and my Facebook group where I suggest further books.

I recommend always carrying a book with you. Or have one on your Kindle and phone so that you can make the most of your time travelling to work on the train or listen to an audio book while driving. Over time you'll work through some interesting books.

If, like me, you're someone who likes to keep a track of everything that you've read then I recommend using the '**Goodreads**' App. There's something so pleasurable about seeing how many books you've read over the year. Or maybe that's just me?!

Exercise 14
Write down three occasions when you can read or listen to an audio book.

1.
2.
3.

Exercise 15
Turn to the list of books that I recommend at the end of this book and write down three that you'd like to read and then either borrow them from your library or go buy them.

1.
2.
3.

Watch motivational videos

Next time you're cooking dinner or going to watch another episode of something on TV put on a TED Talk video instead. You can select the video by topics ranging from adventure to fear to women. They last from four to twenty minutes. The talks may inspire you, give you ideas to try out or simply expand your knowledge.

For a list of my recommended TED Talks to help inspire you check out my blog on my website and Facebook page.

Exercise 16
Write down 3 occasions that you can watch a TED Talk

1.
2.
3.

Exercise 17
Check out the list of TED Talks that I recommend on my blog and write down three that you'd like to watch. Download them so that you can watch them the next time you have a few minutes free.

1.
2.
3.

Personal development courses

I've been on quite a few personal development courses and conferences and I'm sure I could spend my whole life and all my money attending them!

Time and money spent on yourself is so rare these days but I do think it's invaluable to invest in yourself. I now attend at least one course or conference every quarter and I would recommend that you invest this time in yourself. You might see if your company will pay for any costs.

The reason I love them is that you are in a room full of like-minded people that you can connect with and learn from. There is usually an amazing buzz which energizes you and gives you that much needed confidence boost.

To make the most of the course make sure that you schedule some time in your diary to connect with anyone that you met at the event. Then put into place any takeaways otherwise you won't see any benefit from attending.

Note of Caution
If you're attending a personal development course then it's hoped you'll return energized about all the things that you're going to change. If you have a partner, they may worry that they aren't part of the changes or are going to get left behind. So be sure to include them in your plans.

Exercise 18
Write down three courses or events that you would like to attend in the next twelve months and add them to your diary.

1.
2.
3.

Goal setting

As far back as I can remember I've been a goal setter.
At school, I set goals regarding the grades I needed to go to university. Once at university it was about getting a good degree so that I could apply for a graduate scheme.

My current goals are all concerned with this book and my online programme 'Get Confident and Accelerate Your Career.'

Everyone says they know the importance and benefits of goals. Yet so many people struggle to:

- Communicate exactly what their goal is
- Why they want to achieve it
- And when they want to have accomplished it by.

In case you aren't yet convinced of the benefits of goal setting, let's remind ourselves of why it's a good idea to have them.

Why setting goals is beneficial

1. Focuses you on what you want to achieve.
2. Helps you turn your vision into a reality.
3. Stops you from procrastinating.
5. Measures progress.
6. Increases motivation as you achieve smaller goals on the way.
7. Can lead to a promotion at work with a salary increase.

I think we can all agree that a promotion at work with a salary increase sounds like a great result if that was your goal. So how do you go about setting a goal?

How to set goals
Setting SMART objectives seems to be the norm now in the workplace but in case you aren't familiar with the format, here's what SMART objectives are:

- **S** – Specific: You indicate who is doing the action, what's happening, when it's happening, why it's happening and how it's happening.

- **M** – Measurable: State the metrics that you'll use to determine whether you've met your objectives. It should be a numeric or descriptive quality that defines quality, quantity, cost, etc.

- **A** – Attainable: Is this goal attainable and within your capabilities?

- **R** – Relevant: Does the goal align with the broader goals of your life and career?

- **T** – Time-bound: Include the date by which you'll achieve the goal.

An example of a SMART goal could be:
I'll achieve an external promotion to HR Director by January 31st 2018 with an increase in salary package of 15 percent. I will have reduced my commute to a thirty-minute walk instead of a forty-five-minute train ride to help improve my overall fitness and mindfulness.

To achieve that goal I will:
- Update my CV and let ten of my contacts on LinkedIn know that I'm looking for a job.
- Connect with five recruitment agencies and attend one networking event every month.
- Spend time researching the company and do a mock interview with a friend who is an HR Director.
- Read a book on how to negotiate because I know I'm not currently a strong negotiator.

What may stop you achieving goals?

Once you've set your SMART goal, it's time to be honest with yourself and think about what may stop you achieving it – what excuses you might put in the way.

List these excuses and write next to each one ways you can get around them so that you are sure you will achieve this goal.

For example, it may be that you want to do a Master's degree but your excuse for not doing one is that you don't have the money.

Write a list of ways that you can increase your income and reduce your spend. For example, to increase your income you may get a flat mate, put your spare room on Air BnB or get a second job.

To reduce your spend you may negotiate a cheaper phone contract or cancel your gym membership and go for a run with a friend in the park. It may also be worth considering asking your company to sponsor your Master's or see if there's a scholarship available.

I'm sure you get the idea that there are ways around the roadblocks that may sabotage your success.

Recognizing them early on and preparing for how you'll overcome them will ensure you stay on track.

Get support

To help you stay on track you could get a coach, join a mastermind group where you're held accountable each week or try asking at work if there's a mentoring programme that you could sign up to.

Reward your successes

As you move towards achieving your goal, make sure you celebrate the smaller steps so that you stay motivated.

For example, if your goal is to get a new job then your first step may have been to update your CV. Once you've done that, reward yourself with drinks out with friends and once you've got your new job with your increased salary, consider booking a well-deserved holiday.

So now you know that it's a good idea to set goals and how to do it, list three goals that you'd like to achieve in the next twelve months.

Exercise 19
Revisit exercise six where you wrote down three goals and see if these are still the three goals that you want to focus on.

Write down three goals that you would like to achieve in the next twelve months.

1.
2.
3.

Exercise 20
What one action can you take to move each of the above goals forward in the next week?

1.
2.
3.

Exercise 21
What one action can you take to move each of the above goals forward in the next thirty days?

1.
2.
3.

Exercise 22
What may stop you achieving your goals and how will you
overcome those obstacles?

1.
2.
3.

Exercise 23
If you've written down that you'd like a new job, then complete this
exercise as well.

1. What five companies do you want to work for and why?
2. What salary and benefits do you want and why?
3. What does your ideal team look like and why?
4. What is the ideal location and commute and why?

Exercise 24
Are you excited about achieving these goals?
Yes No

If you've circled 'No' to feeling excited about achieving these goals,
then spend some time thinking about why you've set this as a goal.

Are you doing it because you feel that you should, due to pressure
from your partner, family, friends or colleagues? If you aren't excited
by a goal then it's less likely that you'll want to work on it. In that
situation, failure to achieve it is almost inevitable. So challenge
yourself to think of a different goal.

Exercise 25
How will you reward yourself as you achieve your goals?

1.
2.
3.

Vision board

Once you're clear on what you're aiming for, write those goals down, update your positive affirmations on your phone and have them visible so that you'll see them daily.

Creating a vision board is another great way to remind yourself of what you are working towards and why. You may want to spend an hour with a heap of magazines and cut out pictures that will help you remember and visualize your goal. Place it on your wardrobe door, phone and laptop screen saver so it's in constant view. Or you might use Pinterest to add images and words and create a vision board that way.

You may have a picture of the salary that you want, the company you want to work for and the house that the new salary will allow you to get.

Exercise 26
Create your own vision board either by cutting out words and pictures from magazines or by copying pictures from Google and adding them to a document. Then put it up somewhere where it's visible to you every day.

Progress not perfection

I did an online business course last year and one of the key messages I took from that was 'Progress not Perfection.'

Women, as a general rule, tend to be perfectionists. Hence, they don't want to send in a piece of work until they're confident it's an excellent piece of work. Men, as a general rule, on the other hand, tend to complete a piece of work and submit it. Then if there's feedback and changes needed, they'll take that on board, resubmit and move on to the second task while women are still on the first.

Exercise 27
What piece of work are you working on at the moment that you could submit now and ask for feedback, rather than spending any more time on it?

1.
2.
3.

Energy Drainers
Do you have friends, colleagues or acquaintances in your life who are energy drainers? These are people that, when you think of seeing them, make you feel tired, less inspired and not looking forward to meeting up with them.

If you do know people like this, it may be time to stop seeing them if you can. Or at least limit the time that you spend with them so that you've got the energy to focus on what you want. This is a bit trickier if they're a work colleague. In this instance, you may need to be creative and work from home one day, hot desk in another team or put the headphones on so that you can concentrate on your work.

Exercise 28
Write down three people who are negative drainers in your life:
1.
2.
3.

Exercise 29
Write down three ways that you can spend less time with them:
1.
2.
3.

On the other hand, do you have friends and work colleagues who inspire and energize you and give you the confidence boost that you need? Think about people who do this and actively ask them for dinner on a more regular basis if they're a friend. Or for lunch or to a brainstorming session if they're a colleague.

Exercise 30
Write down three positive people that you want to spend more time with and put a date in your diary:
1.
2.
3.

Anchoring

I learnt about the power of anchoring when I got my Neuro-Linguistic programming (NLP) coaching qualifications and now use it with most of my clients. I like the fact that you can anchor any positive feeling and then recall or reactivate that feeling at any time you need it in the future without anyone else knowing.

You may want to anchor a feeling of calm, love, confidence, relaxation, happiness and positivity so that when you stand up in front of your team these feelings support you.

Below is how to anchor any positive feeling that you want. I have confidence anchored to one of my knuckles so when I get outside my comfort zone and feel that I need a boost, I can reactivate the feeling of confidence and get on with the task at hand.

1.   Get comfortable on a chair with your feet on the ground and in a place where you won't be disturbed for ten minutes.
2.   Take a deep breath in and let your whole body relax.
3.   Let all the muscles in your body relax and take a deep breath in again.
4.   If you've still got some tension in your body then take another deep breath in and tighten your muscles and as you breathe out relax all the muscles and feel the tension slip away.
5.   Decide on what positive feeling you want to anchor to be able to recall at a later time.
6.   Close your eyes (having read the below and remembered what you are doing or record the below on to your phone so that you can follow without checking the book)
7.   Remember a time when you were totally - **insert feeling**?
8.   Go back to that time and see what you saw, hear what you heard, feel what you felt and really feel the feelings of being totally - **insert feeling**.
9.   Allow that feeling of - **insert feeling** - to go all the way through your body and make that feeling of -**insert feeling** - bigger, bolder and brighter.
10.   Intensify the - **insert feeling**.

11.   Anchor in the positive feeling by pressing your right thumb onto your ring finger knuckle and holding for a few seconds.
12.   Continue to allow that feeling of - **insert feeling** - go all the way through your body and make that feeling of - **insert feeling** - bigger, bolder and brighter.
13.   Release the thumb and finger.
14.   Think about anything else, such as what you had for breakfast, to break your state.
15.   Repeat this exercise ten times.
16.   Break state after each time.
17.   Test the anchor by imagining a time in the future when you may be in a situation and you want to feel - **insert feeling**. Think about what is different now?
18.   If you aren't able to recall the feeling then that's okay. Either repeat the exercise again or try using a different memory. The one you've used may link to another feeling that's stronger than the one that you're trying to anchor.

Exercise 31
Have fun anchoring all those amazing positive feelings that you want to recall in the future!

Summary of tips to increase your confidence

Congratulations on finishing section two of this book. If you've been doing all the exercises as you read the book, you will be feeling more confident.

Below is a summary of what we've covered. If you haven't completed the exercises then you may want to the take the time now to return and complete them before moving to section three.

1. Turn off the inner voice
     Write an achievements list
     Write a gratitude list
     Practice meditation
     Add positive affirmations to your phone
     Hire an executive coach
     Get outside your comfort zone
2. Read
3. Watch motivational videos
4. Attend personal development courses
5. Set your goals
6. Create your vision board
7. Remember progress not perfection
8. Surround yourself with positive people
9. Anchor two positive states

As we come to the end of section two take time to reflect and complete this last exercise before moving on to section three.

Exercise 32
Think about what you're going to start, stop and keep doing.

Write down three things that you're going to keep doing:
1.
2.
3.

Write down three things that you're going to start doing:
1.
2.
3.

Write down three things that you're going to stop doing:
1.
2.
3.

Section 3

Be More Confident
In the Job

Section 3: In the job

In the previous section, we looked at ways to increase your feelings of confidence in everyday life.

In this section, we explore what practical steps you can take to accelerate your career. Whether that's in your current role or to put into place if you decide to move on.

Mentor

A mentor tends to be someone who has more experience and who can support you and your career. Having said that we're now seeing more 'reverse mentoring' where graduates are being paired up with a senior manager and it's the graduate doing the mentoring.

A mentor may be someone that you know within your company who can look out for you or suggest your name at meetings when managers are discussing succession planning.

In terms of finding a mentor you can ask your line manager and the HR department if there is a formal mentoring programme in place. If not, ask if they can recommend someone. If you're at a small company then you may need to think about who could become your mentor in your wider network.

Exercise 33

Think about who could you ask to become your mentor:

1.
2.
3.

Before you then ask someone to become your mentor, ask yourself the following questions.

Exercise 34

1. What do I want from my mentor? Do I have a specific challenge, issue, or goal that I'd like support with?
2. How often do I want to meet?
3. Where can we meet? Is it in person or on the phone?
5. Why would they want to mentor me?
6. Will I send an agenda or information before the meeting so they know what I want to discuss?
8. How long do I want the relationship to last? Is it to achieve a certain goal or for twelve months and then review?

You may also wish to consider becoming a mentor yourself as you will learn so much from the experience.

Get an executive coach

I know I'm a coach and so I would say this. But I can't stress enough how much it helps having someone who will support you in overcoming that inner voice and work out what's holding you back from achieving your full potential.

Talk to your director or HR Department and ask if your company has an executive coach. If it does, then ask if you can have some sessions with them. If they don't have one then consider hiring one yourself as it will make a huge difference.

Before you meet them, have a think about why you want a coach and how you and the company will benefit.

Exercise 35
1. Why do you want a coach?
2. Is there an issue, problem, challenge or goal that you would like help with? Be prepared to answer why your manager can't help with this.
3. Is there a coach that you've met and would like to work with?
4. If so, how long do you want to see this coach for? Do they have the capacity to take you as a client?
5. How often do you want to see a coach? Once a week or once a month?
6. Will you meet face to face or via Skype?
7. What will be different after the coaching sessions?
8. How will you and the company know if it has been a success?
9. What are the benefits for you and the company? (See the list below which will help you build a business case.)

Those clients who come to me because they have a specific problem often finish our sessions with the observation that if they'd signed up to an executive coach sooner, then they might have been able to prevent the problem in the first place. And THAT would have saved them a lot of energy and anxiety.

The benefits to the individual
- Preparation for role/career changes and joining the board
- Enhancing personal impact and performance
- Improved leadership and management skills
- Increased productivity
- More effective working relationships
- Increased revenue through more focused action
- Greater integrity in managing and decision making
- Fewer negative effects of stress
- Better balance between personal and professional life
- Improved career planning
- Greater confidence
- Focus on solutions rather than problems
- Break through any barriers holding them back
- Develop greater awareness and understanding
- Understand and navigate their interpersonal relationships
- Gain clarity and learn to think creatively
- Deal with change

The benefits to the organization
- Greater commitment from employees
- More creative outlook in business planning
- Improved management of other staff
- Improved revenues and profits
- Improved organizational performance
- Retention of high performers and greater staff loyalty
- Less absenteeism
- Enhanced operational efficiency and flexibility
- Improved staff morale and motivation
- More effective development and performance of new team members
- Unleashing of team potential and improvement in their efficiency and performance

Making the coaching a success

Whether you or the company are paying you'll want to make it a success. Find below some tips to help you get the most from the coaching and make it a successful investment in terms of money and time.

- **Feedback**
  This is a two-way process. If something isn't working then tell the coach – they aren't mind readers. If you feel that you're being pushed too much or not enough then give them this feedback. The more honest you can be with your coach the more they can help you and the more you will get from the sessions.

- **Commit**
  Once you've put the coaching sessions in your diary commit to this time. Block out time before and after if you can so that you can be in the right mindset for the session. There's nothing worse than worrying that you need to rush to a meeting straight after.

- **Action**
  You'll most likely have agreed what action you're going to take from the session. Commit to doing this so that you don't just talk about it for an hour and then fail to follow up. This is where you'll see the real change so take action!

Talk to your Manager

Does your boss know how good you are? I'm guessing not. I bet that you have your head down at your computer getting on with the work, presuming that your boss will know what you're working on and how good you are?

You should be having regular meetings with your manager so that you can share what you've been working on, what you've achieved so far and have the opportunity to ask for feedback. If you're not, then book those meetings now. How else will you know what you're doing well and what you need to improve on?

Don' t wait till your annual appraisal to talk to your manager about where you want to be in a year's time. Sit down with them and share where you want to be and ask them for their help in achieving that.

Exercise 36
1. Where do I want to be in a year?
2. How can my manager help me achieve my goals?
3. How can I help my manager help me achieve my goals?
4. What do I need from my manager?

Talk to your HR Department

My background is in Human Resources so I would recommend having a meeting with your HR representative to explain that you're open to, and looking for opportunities for self development. You never know when they'll be in a meeting and a manager in another team needs extra resources and they think of you.

Exercise 37
1. What support do I need from HR to help me achieve my goals?
2. What help can I offer the HR team that may in return help me in the future?

Ask for feedback

Speak to your manager and HR ask them for feedback on what you should continue to do, or if there's anything that you should stop or start doing.

Exercise 38
1. Who can you ask for feedback?
2. How will you ask for feedback?
3. What feedback did you get?
4. How do you feel about this feedback?
5. What will you change having received this feedback?

Every time you receive feedback, even if you don't agree with what you're told, treat it is a learning opportunity. Take the time to reflect, be kind to yourself and see how you can take this information on board.

Secondment and Projects

If you completed the goal setting activity in section two and now have a clear idea of what you want to achieve in your career then you may have realized that you have a skill gap. Doing a secondment or taking on a project may be the opportunity that you need to learn different skills.

A secondment or project can give you a new challenge and opportunity to learn new skills which will help you close any gaps on your CV. If you're working in a different team or even a different country, then take advantage of the excellent exposure and networking opportunities that this gives you.

You may find that you enjoy the new area, industry, team and location and prefer to stay once the secondment or project has ended. Or you may return to your old team having gained experience in a new area and with a new perspective and with potential collaboration with the new and old teams.

If you do take on a secondment or project, before you start, take time to think about:

Exercise 39
1. What do I want to learn from this opportunity?
2. What achievements and skills do I want to add to my CV?
3. Who do I want to meet and build a relationship with?
4. What do I want to be different at the end?
5. How do I want to feel at the end?
6. Where do I want to go at the end of the secondment or project?

If you're hoping to go for a promotion or change role/industry in the next twelve months then you may need different skills to be able to do the job you're aiming for.

Although you won't be able to do all of the job, it's worth going through the job description of the role that you want. Write down examples alongside the competencies that you can do and highlight the ones that you can't. Then make an action plan of how you can start to learn some of these skills so that you're better prepared when the role becomes available.

Caution
Should you be offered a secondment or project, take time to ensure it's the right opportunity for you and your career. If you can, ask a few people you trust if they think this will be a good opportunity for you or is it a task that no-one else wants?

Do you stay or go?

If you're reading this book then I'm guessing that you may be thinking about either:
- Staying in your current company and trying for promotion.
- Looking at opportunities outside the company

For some this will be a simple decision because there's no way for you to progress where you are. Or it might be that your relationship with your boss has reached a point where the thought of staying one more day makes your heart sink.

For some of you though, this may be one of the hardest career decisions that you make. This is especially true if you enjoy working with your team, have a boss who empowers you and you like the values of the company. Or you simply enjoy the flexible working it offers and the short commute.

Complete the exercise below which will give you clarity and confidence in your decision to stay or look at opportunities outside your current company. It is always worth remembering that if you're offered a role outside, you don't have to take it!

Exercise 40
1. Why am I thinking of leaving?
2. What three things do I enjoy most about my current role?
3. What three things do I enjoy most about my current company?
4. What three things frustrate me about my role?
5. What three things frustrate me about my current company?
6. What role I am looking for in the next twelve months?
7. What salary am I looking for?
8. What other flexible benefits are important to me?
9. What three values are most important to me?
10. How long do I want my commute to be?
11. What do I want my boss and team to be like?
12. Do I prefer a small or global company?
13. Am I happy to travel nationally or internationally for work?
14. Do I want to manage a team?

Volunteer

Volunteering is a great way to learn skills that you may not be able to learn or get exposure to in the work place.

Your company may have a volunteering program where you can take four days a year to volunteer. I recommend taking this opportunity up and consider arranging it alongside colleagues so it becomes a team building day as well. Consider doing:

- A skills day at a local school where you talk about your job/jobs.
- Interview practice
- Painting a school or community centre

The opportunities are endless but so worthwhile.

Exercise 41
1. Does my company run any volunteer programmes?
2. Does my company offer volunteering days?
3. Can I run a volunteer project with my team?
4. If I wanted to volunteer outside of my company, what sort of organization would I like to help?
5. What skills can I offer?
6. What are the gaps on my CV that volunteering may help close?

Be more productive at work
If you've been working through all of the exercises in the book, you should be feeling more confident and putting in place actions that you can do at work to help accelerate your career.

We're now pulled in more directions than ever and below are some ways to ensure that you're more productive at work and not just going round in circles.

Turn off social media
Facebook, LinkedIn, Twitter, Instagram and Pinterest are the biggest time wasters ever! Yes, they are helpful in keeping in touch with friends and family. But if you aren't careful you can lose hours in posting pictures, liking friends' status, retweeting posts and congratulating people on their new baby or job.

It's great to know what's going on in the world and to keep up with everything that's happening in your friend's lives but it doesn't help you to complete your to do list. Research shows that switching tasks can lead to more stress and frustration as you struggle to get everything done. Also, it can take up to twenty-three minutes to become focused again on the task that you were doing before you interrupted yourself. The more complex the task, the longer it will take you to refocus.

I'm going to take a guess that you're something like me. So, I recommend that you only check your phone at a specified time such as when you go grab a coffee, take your lunch break or are commuting home. Unless of course you drive – in which case wait till you're home! Otherwise, to avoid temptation, leave it in your handbag in your drawer at work.

Exercise 42
When does your social media distract you and what can you do to stop checking it?
1.
2.
3.

Action list
At the end of each day do a brain dump for five minutes or less.
Write a list of everything that you have to achieve the next day and
prioritise it. This will help you capture everything that you need to do
so that you don't wake up at 2am worried that you've forgotten to do
something vital.

Exercise 43
Set a reminder on your work computer to come up ten minutes
before you finish work. That way you can write down everything that
you need to do the next day.
1.
2.
3.

Block out time
Once you've made your action list, schedule these activities
into your diary. It may be that the first and last hour of every day is
best for clearing your email inbox and making any phone calls.

If you're a morning person then you may find that first thing is the
best time to do any strategic or big project work as you'll feel more
alert then. Towards the end of the day you may do more
administration tasks when you're feeling less creative.

When I was doing a lot of recruitment in my last corporate HR job I
used to schedule a whole morning on a Friday to make briefing
calls with recruitment agencies. This practice helped me block out
my diary and clump tasks together so that I could focus on that one
task. And it helped my colleagues know that on Friday mornings I
would be on the phone and wouldn't be able to help them till lunch
time. You may want to try something similar.

Exercise 44
Block out time in your diary to mirror your action list:
1.
2.
3.

Eat that frog
If you haven't read the book "Eat That Frog" by Brian Tracey then I recommend that you do. It's got some great tips that you can quickly action to become more productive. The book talks about getting the hard things done first so that you're motivated and focused to do everything else, knowing that you've accomplished the most difficult/unpleasant tasks of the day.

Exercise 45
What activity are you putting off? Put this in your diary now.
1.
2.
3.

Take a break
Do you take your lunch break? 'No, of course I don't' is the usual reply. Followed by 'I'm far too busy' or 'It's not encouraged in my office' or 'I'll be at work even later at the end of the day if I take a break'.

If you're the one in five who does take a lunch break then well done you. I hope that your colleagues learn from you as I imagine that you're a lot more focused than they are in the afternoon.

If you currently aren't taking a lunch break then it's time to reassess that situation and claim back your break.

The benefits of a lunch break, even if it's only for twenty minutes, can make a huge difference to your afternoon's productivity. Which makes it a shame that so many people work in a culture that frowns on lunch breaks. Or, worse still, where not taking them is seen as something commendable – like saying 'I'm far too busy and important to have a lunch break.'

If you need more convincing then here is a reminder of what the benefits of taking a lunch break are.

- **Increased energy**

By taking a break, especially if you're able to get some fresh air and exercise, you avoid that afternoon slump so common at about 3pm. This is when the typical lunch of sandwich, crisps and a chocolate bar results in energy levels plummeting and a struggle to stay awake rather than getting work done.

- **Higher productivity**

As you benefit from an increase in energy you'll find that you're more productive. This is because your concentration levels have increased making it easier to focus on your work. If you've been lucky enough to get a walk around a park, you may find this a good time to do any creative work.

- **Team building**

Should you go out for lunch with your colleagues, this gives you an opportunity to build on your relationship with them and form stronger connections with those that you share the office with.
If you've been working on a project in the morning that you're struggling with then you could ask for their help or opinions and perhaps brainstorm some ideas that you hadn't considered. They may have experienced similar problems and you could find that, when you return to your desk, you have the solution.

- **Fresh perspective**

By taking a break you can return to your desk with a fresh pair of eyes. That way you'll find it easier to spot any mistakes you may have made on any drafts you were working on. Plus, you'll have a clearer idea of what decisions you need to make to complete your work that afternoon.

- **Try new places**

If you're going out with your colleagues, as well as building a stronger team relationship, lunchtime might be a good opportunity to try any new restaurants near the office. And there's the added benefit of taking the time to enjoy your food. Isn't that better than a hastily eaten BLT at your desk? Or worse still, devouring the contents of the biscuit tin. There's a road to piling on the pounds if ever there was one.

- **Back to nature**

If you're lucky enough to work near a park then lunch is the perfect time to get some fresh air and exercise. It will help improve your afternoon mood and concentration levels and reduce your stress levels. Invite your colleagues along with you and you can get fit together.

If you're managing a team, then encourage everyone to take a break. You may find that you notice reduced sickness and lower turnover as you have happy staff and an improvement in customer service. With these benefits, can you afford not to take a lunch break?

Still not convinced? Why not give it a try every day next week and see the benefits for yourself. Go for lunch with colleagues, go for a walk together - ideally in a park. Read a book, do a spinning or yoga class if there's a gym nearby and enjoy taking a break and the benefits that come with it in the afternoon.

Put it in the diary and start tomorrow. Don't feel guilty that you're taking a break and do grab your whole team so that you can all benefit.

Change your mindset

If you're someone that tells yourself that you'll leave work when you've completed everything then I would take a guess that you probably don't leave the office before 7pm.

But try changing your mindset and saying to yourself that you're going to get all your work done by 5.30pm every night because you're going to meet friends, go home and see the kids or go to the gym. That way you'll make an extra effort to get everything done and be out of the office by 5.30pm.

Research shows that we can make work expand to fill as long a day as we want. And I think that we can all agree we don't want to be in the office at 8pm every night. So, start telling yourself you're leaving at 5.30pm.

A favourite tactic of mine that you might try is this: I sometimes treat a day as if I'm going on holiday the next day for a month and have to get everything done that day. Whenever I do this I always manage to cross off so much on my 'To do' list!

Environment
Your working environment can make a big difference to your productivity at the office. Take a few minutes to assess your current office set up and see if there are any changes that you need to make.

1. Make sure that your chair and desk are at the right height. If you can work at a variable desk, try standing for a few hours every day – you'll really notice the difference. I tend to sit at my desk in the morning and then stand in the afternoon. This helps me stay more alert - especially at 3pm when I find my energy levels are at their lowest.

2. If you're allowed pictures in your office then have one of a nature scene. Research shows this will help calm you.

3. Try and shut out noise as much as you can or have a white noise playing in the background. This will help you zone out the other noise in the office.   I use the website **Calm** and have their mountain lake noise playing on my computer. It has the added benefit of being nice to look at on your screen when you're on the phone.

Personal well being

Looking after yourself will make a big difference to your wellbeing. This in turn will help you to be more productive at work.

- Get exercise – if you can, get at least thirty minutes of exercise every day. You'll really notice a difference in your work productivity. Perhaps when the weather is good, why not invite your colleagues to go for a walk together at lunchtime? This way you're getting exercise while building stronger relationships with your team.

- It's important to get up and move occasionally so set a reminder on your computer and every ninety minutes get out of your chair - even it's only to walk to the printer or top up your water glass.

- Decide on what time you want to go to sleep and set an alarm clock for thirty minutes before so that you can start to get ready. If you aren't convinced you need more sleep then read 'The Sleep Revolution: Transforming Your Life, One Night at a Time' by Arianna Huffington. Trust me, after reading her book you will be getting more sleep and feel so much better for doing so.

Nutrition

Looking after your body by being aware of what you're drinking
and eating will help you maintain your energy and concentration
levels. Try drinking at least two litres of water a day, eating a great
brain boosting breakfast and having healthy snacks by your desk
such as fruit, cut up vegetables and nuts. If you haven't yet listened
to my podcast with Claire Stone, a nutritionist, then you can listen to
it on my podcast show.

Exercise 46
What three things will I stop doing to help me be more productive?
1.
2.
3.

Exercise 47
What three things will I start doing to help me be more productive?
1.
2.
3.

Ask for a pay rise

Asking for a pay rise can be a daunting and nerve -
wracking experience. It may be something that you put off, waiting
and hoping for your employer to recognize your amazing
contribution to the company.

However, I would recommend that you take the bull by the horns
and have the discussion with your manager.

By following the tips below you may find yourself with a fantastic
pay rise. So book in that meeting!

Timing
Before you ask your manager for a meeting consider when is the
best time for you both to sit down undisturbed.

In most work places this would mean Monday mornings are best
avoided because your boss may well be firefighting. Conversely
Friday afternoon is probably not a great time either as your boss
will, in all likelihood, be winding down for the weekend.

If your team is working towards a deadline and a big pitch then
avoid this period too. You want your boss to be as relaxed as
possible with time to listen to you, so consider having the meeting
after lunch.

Research
Before you go and ask for a 20 percent increase do your market
research. Check that your role in your industry is paying this
externally. If it isn't then prepare to justify why you think your role
deserves the increase.

Be prepared
When you have your meeting with your line manager, say that you'd
like to discuss your salary. Explain that you've made a note of your
justifications for this request and that you'd like to go through it with
them if they are agreeable.

Reasons you could use to support your request for a pay increase might be:

- Your role is not aligned with the market rate for the same or broadly similar work.
- Your role has taken on more responsibility.
- The addition of a new geographic area to your area of responsibility.
- You've taken on new line management responsibilities.

Be armed with any relevant facts and figures so that, if your boss asks any questions, you can respond immediately.

Dress code
I always tell my clients 'dress for the job you want, not the job that you have'. You want to make a good impression at this meeting so as well as having your list of justifications for your request, consider what you wear to the meeting.

Follow up with an email
I believe that it's always good practice to send an email after the meeting thanking your manager for their time and giving a summary of what you discussed. If you agreed a date by which they'd get back to you then add this to the email.

Ignore personal reasons
When asking for a pay rise stick to the facts in relation to your job and don't mention that you need to buy a new car and that this increase would allow you do that. Needing a new car, holiday or mortgage is not a valid reason to ask for a pay rise and may make your line manager question your professionalism.

Feedback
If, for any reason, your manager refuses your request for a rise, ask them for feedback on why this is.

Clarify with your manager what you need to do in the next few months to be considered for an increase. Ask too for a salary review in six months' time.

Once you've had this discussion follow it up with an email confirming all the details. If you've agreed to review it again in another six months' time then add this to the email.

Exercise 48
1. Is it the right time to ask for a pay rise?
2. What has changed?
3. What is the market salary for your role?
4. When and where will you ask to meet your manager?
5. What is your business case for a raise?

Say no

On being asked to undertake a task or take on something extra, most people find saying 'no' really hard to do. And I include myself here. People find saying 'no' difficult because they don't like conflict and because they want to help people. Hence, they often find themselves saying 'yes' when it's not what they mean at all.

Saying 'yes' can lead to great opportunities and meeting some fantastic people but it can also be exhausting!

The problem we have at work is that we want others to see us as a team player. We don't want to appear boring or difficult to work with.

But, if we always acquiesce, then we can end up feeling pressured, or maybe even bullied, and that will lead to feelings of resentment. Conversely, if we do refuse a request, we can feel guilty and worried that we might have offended someone.

It's a minefield, but one that you can navigate with success. If you find yourself agreeing to do things you don't want to more often than you should, then it may be time to take back some time for yourself.

This quote from Warren Buffett may help you to say 'no': 'The difference between successful people and really successful people is that really successful people say no to almost everything'.

Tips for saying no at work

Reframe
When you find yourself wanting to answer 'yes' to something, stop and think about what that 'yes' actually means in terms of what it would displace that you would rather be doing. It will help you reframe and learn to say 'no' more easily, swiftly and, more importantly, without the guilt.

Offer an alternative
If you can't start a project at work this week maybe you can offer to start it next week?

Take time to consider the request
Assess the pros and cons before you refuse to take on a piece of work your boss has requested that you do. Consider if it will it help you with your overall career goals. Will it be a good opportunity to network, increase your salary or gain exposure to a different team? If it helps with any of these goals then it may be in your interests to take it on for its wider benefits.

Say no in person
If you're able to refuse someone's request face-to-face then the message is likely to be better received, as the wrong impression or tone can be given in an email.

Ask for help prioritizing
Ask your boss if you need help prioritizing your workload. Discuss together what can either be postponed for a few days or delegated to another team member. It's even possible that such a discussion might bring about the realization that actually, this 'thing' is no longer required.

Practise
If you're normally a 'yes' person, then start small or practise with friends or family.
Once you've said 'no' a few times you'll get more confident with it. And what's more you'll start to enjoy the benefits of having some more time to say 'yes' to the things that you *do* want to do.

Exercise 49
1. What have you agreed to in the last month that you wish you hadn't?
2. Why did you say yes?
3. Do you have any appointments in your diary over the next month that you don't want to attend and don't have to? If so, send your apologies and cancel.

Section 4

Looking for

a

new job

Section 4: Looking for a new job

If you've worked through the other sections in the book, you may have made the decision that you're ready for a new job within the next twelve months.

Congratulations if you're ready. Take some time to celebrate your realization that you're ready for that next step and are prepared to go get it.

But if you aren't feeling ready spend some time thinking about whether that's genuine. Or is it more that you need to do some more confidence exercises to remove the inner voice that's sabotaging your success and preventing you from stepping outside your comfort zone?

So, what next? If you've decided to go for a new role within your current company, you may still need to update your CV, network outside of your department and secure the role through an interview.

Alternatively, you may have decided to move on from your current company. In which case updating your CV, LinkedIn profile, connecting with recruitment agencies and feeling confident at interviews will be your next steps.

So, work through section four as you never know what opportunities are around the corner.

CV

I saw thousands of CVs in my HR career and it never failed to surprise me that they could be so bad that I didn't want to spend any time reading through them.

From being six pages long to tons of spelling and grammar mistakes and cover notes stating the wrong job title or, even worse, the wrong company name.

Work through the suggestions below to update your CV and remember progress not perfection - you can always make further changes later.

List your achievements
When you're updating your CV, it would seem obvious that the first step would be to sit down with your current one and amend from there. But, I would recommend not looking at your CV at all until you've first brainstormed your achievements.

To do this get a plain piece of paper and set the timer for thirty minutes. That's so you don't procrastinate and find yourself three hours later still there worrying what you've missed. Instead start by brainstorming all of the achievements that come to mind.

You'll find that once you start writing, the achievements will start to flow. Start with your current role and then work backwards. Once you've done this go through your performance appraisals, your email folders and your diary and write down any accomplishments that you've missed during the brainstorming session.

That done, you can start to include these achievements in your current CV. You'll want to ensure that you highlight key figures such as 'increased sales by 20 percent, reduced costs by 10 percent or ' recruited ten people every month'.
The number of accomplishments you have may depend on how long you've been in that role. So, if you've been with a particular

company for a year then you may only have three bullet points. But if you've been with them for ten years then you might have seven achievements that you want to state.

I would recommend that, above all, you make the CV no longer than two pages.

Be truthful
If you've said that you led a team of fifty then have ready examples of how you did this, what your successes and challenges were and what you learnt.

If you've lied on your CV then be sure it will come out – maybe not at interview but definitely once you are in the job. And then it's simply uncomfortable for everyone and you risk losing your job and your reputation in the market.

Tailor your CV
Read the job description thoroughly and make sure somewhere on your CV you've covered all the requirements as best you can.

If there's a skill on the job description that you don't have then that's absolutely fine – but think about how you'll learn that skill once you start so that it's not a problem for the recruiting company. Or, if it comes up in the interview, you're prepared.

Vary the vocabulary
I've seen CVs where each line begins with the terms 'managed', 'implemented' or 'introduced'. This shows lack of imagination and laziness so don't do it! You can download a free list of power words that I recommend to include. It's on my website here: www.carolinearnoldcoaching.com/resources

Edit
According to research, 20 percent of hiring managers will dismiss a CV due to a spelling mistake and 98 percent of hiring managers will dismiss if there's more than one. It's vital then to make sure that you've proofread your CV. Ask a friend to do a final check too.

If you're thinking about applying for a new job, whether internally or externally, you'll only have seconds to impress the hiring manager/ recruitment consultant/HR team. So, it's important you get it right the first time otherwise you'll simply waste your time and theirs.

Exercise 50
1. Brainstorm for 30 minutes and write down as many achievements that you can think of.
2. Review the last few years' appraisals and add these achievements to your brainstorming document.
3. Scan your email folders and diary to check that you haven't missed anything and add if applicable.
4. Prioritise your list of achievements and list no more than five in each job.
5. Download the free CV template from my website.
6. Update your CV including the content you've now collated.
7. Download the CV Power words from the website and ensure you aren't starting every sentence with 'introduced'. www.carolinarnoldcoaching.com/resources
8. Ask a friend to proofread to ensure there are no mistakes.

LinkedIn

There are now 500 million users on LinkedIn making it the world's largest professional network. Hence if you're thinking of changing jobs it's a great tool to use on a consistent basis.

Every time I've thought about moving roles my first port of call was LinkedIn. It's an invaluable professional platform that can increase your network and may help you get a new job.

Work through the below suggestions to update your LinkedIn profile and be open to invites to connect as you never know what may come of them. Obviously, if you don't feel comfortable with a request then you can decline the invite as well as blocking them if you wish.

Settings
Before you make any changes to your profile you may want to consider editing your settings so that your connections aren't alerted to every change that you make. Remember though, just before you do the last edit, to turn on the alert setting again. That way people will get a notification that you've made a change and feel inspired to click on your new updated profile.

Photo
My advice is to use a professional photo. Using a good professional photo on your profile reputedly makes you fourteen times more likely to be found on LinkedIn.

I've heard that some recruitment agencies won't even click on your name if you don't have a photo as they presume the profile is not current. So don't be one of those people.

If you don't want to invest in a professional photo then ask a friend to take a picture in front of a plain background.

While you're updating your LinkedIn photo it's a good idea to double check your other social media channels and update if necessary. Photos of you at a wedding with your arm around a friend with a glass of Champagne are fine for Facebook but not appropriate for LinkedIn.

Connections
Connect with as many relevant people as possible. You never know who their connections might be and who they might be able to introduce you to.

LinkedIn makes it easy to search for people by your current company or ex-colleagues, school and university. You can then see if there's anyone you'd care to connect with on a professional basis.

Profile and summary
If you're short on time then you can copy your content from your CV but if you've got different material do use that instead. But remember you can edit the profile at any time so there's no need to spend all day on it in the first instance.

Testimonials
Draw up a list of possible people that you could ask to write a testimonial for you. These could be customers, clients, managers, and colleagues. Email them individually asking if they can write you a testimonial for your time at X workplace and offer to write them one in return. You may want to suggest a format for them to complete such as: How well you knew each other, what you helped them to achieve, what effect you had on them or their business and what's better now as a result of the work you did.

Contact details
Your details will only be available to your connections but make sure they are up-to-date so it's simple for people to contact you.

Education
Although it may be a while since you left university, it's worth updating these details and reconnecting with school and university

friends. They may be in companies that you'd love to work for or vice versa.

Job Title

It's important to spend some time thinking about your job title on LinkedIn. This may be the first thing that the recruitment manager may search for, so you want to ensure that you come up.

You may think that you just have the one title, for example HR Director. But you may also put Head of Change, recruiting talent, and employee engagement along with what regions you cover whether UK or international. If you aren't sure what to put, have a search for other HR Directors and see what they've done to give you some ideas.

Exercise 51

1. Update your LinkedIn photo.
2. Connect with family, friends, school, university and colleagues.
3. Update your profile including summary, contact details and education.
4. Contact five people and ask them for a testimonial.

Networking

I'm sure that you've heard the saying 'it's not what you know but who you know'. If you're job searching then this couldn't be truer.

When I moved to Bristol I threw myself into networking as I didn't know anyone. I've found that networking is a great way to meet new people, help you land your next fantastic role or potentially meet someone that you would like to become your mentor.

If you're new to networking the thought of starting it can be a daunting one. So work through the below exercises and start to grow your network.

Before The Event

Elevator pitch
If this is your first networking event then I suggest you spend some time on your elevator pitch before you go. Your elevator pitch should last no more than 60 seconds and explain what you do. I tweak the message depending on the audience and tailor my 'ask' to suit what I currently need. The more specific you can be the better as it does help the audience to help you.

If you know the company that you want to work for then ask for an introduction to it in your ask. You never know who's in the audience or who someone *in* the room knows *outside* the room.

Be prepared
You may read the following and think 'those are obvious'. But it's surprising how many don't get it right.
- Know where you're going and what time the event starts.
- Check train times, congestion charges and parking.
- Have a strategy of what you'd like to get out of networking i.e. grow your network and find a new job.
- Take plenty of business cards and consider having copies of your CV.

Guest list
Contact the organizer to ask if you can have a copy of the guest list. Spend some time going through it and highlighting who you want to meet at the event. That way, when you arrive at the networking event, you can ask the organizer if they can possibly introduce you to the person that you'd most like to meet.

Exercise 52
1. What event can you attend in the next month and add it to your diary.
2. What will you say during your elevator pitch?

During the Event

Arrive early
When you go to a networking event make a point of arriving early as that creates opportunities for introducing people to each other as they arrive – something they are often grateful for if they're new to networking.

First impressions count
You only have a few seconds to make that first impression so get it right!

Remember:
- Make eye contact
- Smile – people will then approach you!
- Dress smartly or at least appropriately for the event
- Have an open and confident body language pose
- Give a firm handshake
- Welcome people into your conversation

If networking doesn't come naturally to you then the tips below will help you start a conversation with anyone.

Small talk
An easy way to start a conversation with someone is to engage the person in small talk.

If there's a holiday coming up try asking them a question about that. Things such as 'What are you doing for summer holidays?' or, if you're meeting them at the beginning of the week, 'How was your weekend?' or alternatively at the end of the week 'What are you doing this weekend?'

Ask for their recommendations
It's flattering to be asked for recommendations. So, if you're attending an event try asking if they've been to the event before. Then, if you get an affirmative answer, you can ask what they recommend seeing or doing. Should you be at a restaurant, try

asking the person/people you are with what they'd recommend from the menu.

Make them feel comfortable
You can do this by asking them a question that's easy for them to answer. If you're at an event you could ask 'Have you been here before?', 'Which talks are you looking forward to?' or 'How was your journey in?'

Ask open-ended questions
If you ask closed questions such as 'Do you like reading?' it's possible you'll get 'no' for an answer. And that's that conversation killed. Instead try asking them what their favourite book is and why they enjoy it so much.

Ask about their kids, partner, holidays, and hobbies
People like to talk about themselves so ask them what they like doing when they aren't networking. And then, if they say it's taking the children to swimming and football, you can follow it up by enquiring how many children they have.

Remark on your surroundings
This is a great way to start a conversation if you're at an event and you're getting a drink as you can turn to the person next to you and comment 'Isn't it a lovely location/room/restaurant?' deleting as applicable.

Give a compliment
Most people love to get a compliment so you could say 'I like your handbag, where did you get it?' Be genuine in your compliments though. If you think it's the most hideous bag you've ever seen it might be better to comment on their shoes instead. A fake compliment will be obvious.

Refer to previous conversations
If you've met the person before but still don't know them that well try asking them about something they were doing last time you met. Something like: 'The last time we met I recall you were off on

holiday to Greece. What was the best bit?' You'll impress people if you remember details about them.

So now that you've got some examples of how to start a conversation let's remind ourselves of the basics when talking to people.

Be approachable
Smile if someone catches your eye because this will make it easier for them to join you.

Relax
Remember that others may be nervous too so just relax and practice starting conversations. That way you get used to doing it without thinking about it.

Say the other person's name from time to time
This will help you remember it for the future and will also help you build rapport with the person.

Acknowledge that you're listening
Let them know that you're listening and interested in what they have to say by nodding your head and making appropriate comments and responses.

After the event

Follow up
The success is in the follow up so spend time going through the guest list and send them an invite to connect on LinkedIn. I now send an invite to people that I met and to those that I wasn't able to meet and simply mention the event we both attended and suggest it would be good to connect.

Plan a long-term relationship
It's not likely that you'll land your dream job after your first networking event. You'll need to show commitment and energy to grow some fantastic long-term relationships. Ask them how you can help them – you never know you may just be able to introduce them to the person they want to meet.

Exercise 53
1. During the event write on the business card something that will allow you to remember them later on.
2. Using the guest list, connect on LinkedIn with those who attended the event.

Recruitment Companies

Recruiters can get a bad name but I've worked with some fantastic ones over the years. All the roles that I had when I was working in HR, in the corporate environment, came through a recruitment consultant. So it's definitely worth building relationships with those in your industry.

Recruiters can give you advice on your CV, the buoyancy of the market and the realism of your salary expectations. They can then look for opportunities on your behalf – roles that you would perhaps not have come across because they weren't advertised on their website or LinkedIn.

List of recruitment companies
It can be quite daunting and time consuming trying to find the right recruitment company to register with so I've saved you some of the leg work and compiled a list of companies.

These are organizations that:
* I've used personally when I was job searching.
* Used when I was recruiting as the HR manager of a company.
* Have heard of but not yet used. With these I recommend that you use your own due diligence before you register with them.

The best way to do this is to visit their website and check that they cover your location, your level of role and have vacancies available.

Visit my website at carolinearnoldcoaching.com/resources to download the list of recruitment companies to get you started.

Connect
Once you've decided which recruitment companies you want to register with send them an invite to connect on LinkedIn. Ask if you can send them your CV then meet them face-to-face.

Meeting recruitment consultants can take some time so you may want to book a day's holiday. That way you won't always have to rush off after work to meet them and make excuses why you must leave at that time.

Exercise 54
1. Write down which recruitment companies and recruitment consultants you want to connect with.
2. Send them an invite to connect on LinkedIn.
3. Book a day's holiday so that you can meet the recruitment consultants without the worry about leaving work on time.

Be open to opportunities
Good recruitment consultants will most likely want to see you face-to-face so that they can get a better understanding of who you are, what you've achieved and what you're looking for. That way, when they meet a client they can provide a true picture of you and your skills and promote you into the right opportunities.

When recruitment consultants call you to discuss an opportunity take some time to consider the role even if it doesn't seem to tick all your boxes straight away. It may be worth meeting the hiring manager to learn more about the role and the company to explore if it's a good opportunity for you and your career.

Say No
If you know the opportunity isn't right for you either at the beginning of the process after reading the job description, or after attending the interview then don't be afraid to say no. Simply explain to the consultant why the role or company isn't right for you at the moment so that they can move on to finding one that is.

Follow up
Recruitment consultants are busy people with large databases of candidates and roles to fill so if you haven't heard from them for a while, or your circumstances have changed, then get in touch with them so that they can update their records.

Interview

I recall an incident about 10 years ago. I was applying for an internal job and I asked colleagues for any advice that might help me prepare for the interview.

The advice I received was to wear a short skirt. Not quite what I was expecting. But rather than responding to it in some way I simply kept my skirt length where it was and went for the interview.

Now, with the benefit of hindsight, I can see that I should indeed have commented. As I think about it now, I can see that it was in fact shocking that someone should say such a thing. However, I didn't want to make a scene and I wanted the job.

Since then I've had numerous job interviews and have also been the interviewer for hundreds of candidates. You can definitely see the difference between the candidates that have prepared for an interview and those that have simply rocked up and not given it much thought.

So, how do you succeed at interview, especially if you haven't had one for a while? Here are some tips to help you to interview success:

Research

Have a look at the profiles of the interviewers and some of their team and senior management. Look for what experience they have, their length of service with the company and if they've either had promotion or made any lateral moves – and how often.

Remember this is a two-way process so you want to know if people are leaving after a year or so or if people stay and get promoted.

Job description

Go through the job description and write down against each competency a couple of examples of when you achieved this. If there are any points where you can't think of anything don't worry – simply think about what training or support you may need to achieve that.

Company

Have a look at their website and familiarize yourself with their accounts. See how many employees there are and what their mission is etc. I remember one interview where the hiring manager's last question was about the company's previous day's share price. Luckily, I knew this. The moral of the story? It's worth spending time getting to know the company.

How will you get there? I recall interviewing a candidate who would have to walk and then take a long train journey. I was sceptical that they could manage the journey every day and be on time. But they'd checked all the options and worked out that, if there was a problem with one method of transport, they had alternative routes. They convinced me this wouldn't be a problem. You may want to consider though if you want a long journey in rush hour every day. If the answer to that is a 'no' then you may want to look for a role closer to your home.

CV

Go through your CV, know the facts and figures that you have stated, the dates when you were at particular companies and be comfortable expanding on any of the achievements listed.

Arrive early

Leave yourself plenty of time to get to the interview. There is nothing worse for an interviewer then meeting a candidate who is hot and sweaty, out of breath and completely stressed out because they were running late.

Instead, help yourself by arriving early and grabbing a coffee nearby so that you go in to the interview relaxed and in a positive frame of mind.

First impressions

- You only get one chance to make a great first impression so make it count.
- Smile – when you see the interviewers, smile at them, you want to appear approachable.
- Make eye contact – this can make you look interested and trustworthy.
- Firm handshake – this can help you look confident.

Give examples

When you answer a question follow it up with a supporting example. That will show the interviewer how you work through problems as well as what experience you have.

Questions and next step

Have a couple of questions prepared. These questions may vary depending on your experience level. If you've come through a recruitment agency they may have answered what sort of role you're going for but think about:

- Why has the position become available?
- What are the main objectives and responsibilities of the position?
- How does the company expect you to meet these objectives?
- What obstacles are commonly encountered in reaching these objectives?
- What is the desired time frame for reaching the objectives?
- What can you expect from them in terms of development and support?
- Where will the job fit into the team structure?
- What's the best thing about working at the company?
- What's the turnover of staff like throughout the company?
- Are there any plans for expansion?
- How would they describe the company culture and management style?

Thank you

It's good practice to send an email or a message on LinkedIn after the interview to thank everyone for their time. You can add in that you're interested in the role and that you look forward to hearing from them.

Exercise 55

Practice your interview skills by answering the questions below:

1. Talk us through your CV
2. What are your strengths and weaknesses?
3. Why do you want to work here?
4. What was your biggest achievement in your last role?
5. What is the biggest frustration in your current role?
6. What has been the biggest challenge in your current role and how did you deal with it?
7. Can you give an example when you have had to influence key stakeholders?
8. Why are you leaving your current role?
9. How would your team and boss describe you?
10. Can you give an example when you have had to negotiate and how you dealt with it?
11. Describe a situation in which you led a team.
12. Describe a situation in which you worked within a team? What was your role?
13. What do you expect to be doing in five years' time?
14. Describe a situation in which you dealt with confrontation.
15. Describe a situation in which you motivated people to meet a tight deadline.
16. Describe a situation in which you used your initiative.
17. Describe a situation in which you had to make a difficult decision.
18. What do you know about the company?
19. What type of work environment do you prefer?
20. What's your management style?
21. If applicable, why was there a gap in your employment?
22. If applicable, can you explain why you changed career paths?
23. What would your first 30/60/90 days look like in this role?
24. Do you have any questions for us?

Reflection

Finding the right new role for you and your career can take time. The process comes with highs and lows so do take time to look after yourself and celebrate when you get news of a job offer.

It may be tempting to accept a job offer straight away - especially if you aren't enjoying your current role. But take some time to ensure that this is the right role for you by completing the exercise below. You don't want to be in a position where you start a new role and quickly realize it isn't the right role, boss or company for you.

Exercise 56

1. Where is the office located and what will the commute be like? Do you want to be doing it every work day for the next year? Or the next ten years?
2. What's the cost of the train ticket, car park etc.?
3. What are the hours like and if they're long do you want to be committing to that at this stage in your career?
4. What is the overall package like including salary, pension, flexible benefits, holiday days, sickness, maternity? Is this everything that you wanted? If not then this is the time to negotiate.
5. Does the company offer flexible working? If so consider asking for it to be added to your contract. For example, can you work one day a week from home?
6. What are the opportunities available in the long term such as secondments, projects, promotion or working abroad?
7. What is the culture like including the values and mission? And do these align with your values?
8. Is it a small or big company? Does it suit your preferences?
9. Is the company growing or stagnant?
10. What is the office lay out like? Is it open plan with hot desk? If so do you like this style?
11. What are the facilities on site available to you and do they appeal? Things such as gym, canteen, bike storage and showers.
12. Does the role involve any travelling? If so, what is the travel policy? Can you book business class if you need to fly to Australia and what are the travel expectations? Will it involve weekends away?
13. What's your boss like? Do they inspire you and seem interested in your development?
14. What's your team like? Will they cause any Sunday blues?
15. What's the senior leadership team like? Is there a diverse board of directors?
16. What are your areas of responsibility?
17. Will you have to join conference calls early or late in the evening?
18. Does this role excite you?

Negotiation

The best time to negotiate your package is on your way in. So, make sure you take some time to understand all the details of your package. If you're unsure of anything or you want to negotiate for more salary or holiday allowance now is your chance.

The company will want to know why you want more so make sure that you're prepared to answer. It may be that you want your current holiday allowance matched or a higher salary to meet the market rate. Alternatively, you may be in a position where you have two offers on the table so you can compare and contrast the offers.

Exercise 57
1. What salary and package do you want? How far off is this offer and what can you do to negotiate it?

Resigning

Perhaps you've handed in your notice many times before? Or is this your first time and you're feeling anxious about how to tell your boss?

Making the decision to leave your job and resign can be an exciting time or it may be something that you're dreading. But however you feel, it's important to know how to hand in your notice in a professional manner. One that enables you to leave the door ajar and that ensures the process is a smooth and amicable one. Below are some simple suggestions to give you confidence in resigning.

Reflect

If you've got another job to go to then I hope you'll have thought about why you want to leave your current company. Please don't ever resign in the heat of the moment. Do that and it's more than likely that you'll regret it the next day. And you may not then be able to retract it.

Face to Face

Tell your boss face to face wherever possible. If they're based in another country then you may have to tender your resignation by a phone call. Not an ideal situation. If you do have to call them, quickly get to the point and then agree to have a follow up call a few hours later. This gives them time to digest the news and you can then put a plan in place together on how to recruit your replacement.

It's good practice to follow up this discussion with an email or letter confirming your conversation with useful information such as when your last day will be and how much holiday you have left to take etc.

Be prepared

During the meeting, or shortly after it, your company may offer you a salary increase to entice you to stay. Before the meeting know how much you're worth and what would make you stay. But don't take offence if you aren't offered an increase. Most companies realize that there's a strong likelihood of you leaving after six months anyway as there's often reasons other than salary behind decisions to leave.

Support

Once you've handed in your notice, offer to help as much as possible. You never know when you may want to go back or have them as one of your clients in the future.

Ask your manager what tasks they'd most like you to complete before you go and to whom you should hand over information. If there isn't an up to date job description for your role then offer to produce one and meet with a number of recruitment companies that you can then recommend to your boss.

Be Professional

The chances are your resignation took your boss and your team by surprise. If you were working on a particular piece of work with them they may begin to panic about delivering it with one team member down. This may result in them getting stressed and displaying some negativity towards you. Please don't take this personally. Such a reaction is actually a compliment towards your contribution. It's important that you remain professional at all times during your notice period.

Exercise 58
1. When will you hand in your resignation?
2. What will you say in the meeting?
3. What will you say in the resignation letter?

Section 5

Resources

Section 5: Books

1. Nice Girls Don't Get the Corner Office: Unconscious Mistakes Women make that Sabotage their Career - Lois Frankel

2 Nice Girls Don't Get Rich: 75 Avoidable Mistakes Women Make with Money - Lois Frankel

3 The First 90 Days - Michael D Watkins

4 Who is in your Personal Boardroom? - Zella King and Amanda Scott

5 The Presentation Secrets of Steve Jobs - Carmine Gallo

6 The Storyteller's Secret - Carmine Gallo

7 Talk Like TED - Carmine Gallo

8 The Miracle Morning - Hal Elrod

9 Lucky Bitch: A Guide for Exceptional Women to Create Outrageous Success - Denise Duffield Thomas

10 Get Rich, Lucky Bitch!: Release Your Money Blocks and Live a First Class Life - Denise Duffield Thomas

11 Lean In: Women, Work and the Will to Lead - Sheryl Sandbery

12 The Glass Elevator: A Guide to Leadership Presence for Women on the Rise - Ora Shtull

13 The Glass Wall - Sue Underman and Kathryn Jacob

Thank you

Thank you for reading this book. I hope that you've enjoyed reading and that it helps you with your career.

Please feel free to connect with me via my social media platforms and share how this book has helped you.

Connect

Website
Visit my site and subscribe to my newsletter
www.carolinearnoldcoaching.com

LinkedIn
Connect with me on LinkedIn to broaden your network
linkedin.com/in/carolinearnoldcoach

Facebook
Like my page https://m.facebook.com/Carolinearnoldcoaching

Twitter
Follow me on Twitter for more career tips @Carnoldcoaching

Instagram
Follow me on Instagram https://www.instagram.com/carolinearnoldcoaching/

About The Author

Caroline Arnold has a range of roles. She is an executive coach, consultant, trainer, mentor, speaker, non-executive director and lecturer.

She uses her wide experience to help women acquire the necessary confidence and self-belief to accelerate their career and fulfil their potential.

Photograph by Janette Edmonds

Printed in Great Britain
by Amazon